FOR MY MOTHER AND FATHER

The text of this book is set in 14-point Bembo.

The illustrations are acrylic paintings, reproduced in full color.

Library of Congress Cataloging-in-Publication Data

Curlee, Lynn.

Into the ice: the story of arctic exploration / written and illustrated by Lynn Curlee.

p.   cm.

Includes bibliographical references

Summary: Describes the ice cap above the northernmost shores of Asia, North America, and Greenland,

and the expeditions that crisscrossed it in search of the North Pole.

ISBN 0-395-83013-3

1. Arctic regions—Discovery and exploration—Juvenile literature. [1. Arctic regions—Discovery and

exploration. 2. Explorers. 3. North Pole—Discovery and exploration.]   I. Title.

G614.C87   1997

998—dc20   96-24125 CIP AC

Printed in Singapore

TWP 10 9 8 7 6 5 4 3 2 1

The ice was here, the ice was there,
The ice was all around:
It cracked and growled, and roared and howled,
Like noises in a swound!
—SAMUEL TAYLOR COLERIDGE
The Rime of the Ancient Mariner

IT IS DAWN at the North Pole. After several weeks of hazy twilight, the sun finally appears on the horizon in mid-March. The North Pole's "day" lasts for the next six months, the sun slowly spiraling higher in the sky until June 21, when it begins descending day by day until sunset in late September. Summer is brief and bright, winter long and dark—a frozen night lasting half a year.

From the Pole, an invisible point marking the northern end of our planet's axis, every direction is south, and for hundreds of miles there is nothing but ice and water. The polar ice cap is made up of individual floes that float on the surface of the frigid Arctic Ocean. Jammed together, they move and shift, colliding and separating to form a weird, rugged, and constantly changing surface. Averaging about twelve feet thick, the ice pack melts slightly under the brilliant sunlight of summer, but as winter approaches it refreezes and advances southward once more. The polar ice cap is one of the bleakest and most treacherous environments on earth.

At its edges, the great expanse of ice grinds against the northernmost shores of Asia, North America, and Greenland. Except for a brief midsummer flowering, the land around the Arctic Ocean appears barren, much of it covered with glaciers and snowfields. In the grip of the bitter arctic winter, it seems completely frozen. Yet the lands and seas that surround the North Pole teem with animal life. There are caribou and musk oxen, hares and weasels, wolves, foxes and polar bears, birds and fish, and the sea mammals—seals, walrus, and great whales.

People live here, too. The last Ice Age ended 10,000 years ago. Following the animals, humans moved into the Arctic. They made clothing, shelter, tools, and weapons from stone, driftwood, and the inedible parts of the animals they killed—tusks, bones, antlers, teeth, sinew, skin, and fur. During the long winter they burned animal fat for heat

An Inuit hunter rows his kayak of driftwood and sealskin.

and light. They called themselves *Inuit,* which means "the people," and for thousands of years they thought they were the only people in the world.

THE FIRST PERSON in history to leave a record of a voyage in the far north was Pytheas of Massalia, a Greek merchant who lived in the fourth century B.C. Looking for sources of tin and amber, he sailed into the Atlantic and turned his galley toward Britain, the edge of the known world. From his account, it appears that Pytheas sailed around the British Isles to another land, six days' sail farther north. He called this fog-shrouded land *ultima Thule,* a phrase meaning "the farthest place known to exist." Pytheas's Thule was probably southern Norway.

Ancient Greeks and Romans thought of the north as a region of frozen wastes, icy winds, and darkness; a place of chaos and terror—the home of uncivilized barbarians. But they also believed that "beyond the north wind" was another land, a pleasant place of plenty with warm breezes and happy people. This attractive idea was kept alive by Christian monks in Ireland during the Dark Ages in Europe. Seeking the fabled Isles of the Blessed, seventeen Irish monks under the leadership of their abbot, Saint Brendan, set sail into the North Atlantic about A.D. 550. Their craft was a carraugh, a long, open, seaworthy boat of oiled oxhide stretched over a light wooden frame. During the course of their voyage the monks encountered an astonishing "crystal castle" in the sea. It was an iceberg. Brendan had them sail through a hole in the iceberg carved by the wind and waves. The ice tunnel looked to the saint like "the Eye of God."

Four hundred years later, sailors from Scandinavia entered the North Atlantic in their longboats. Some Norsemen were Viking raiders, but many were settlers who established small outposts in Iceland, Greenland, and a place called Vinland in North

Saint Brendan encounters an iceberg.

America. But the small, far-flung settlements failed and the people died out. Eventually the early voyages in the far north were remembered only in legends.

A great age of geographical exploration began with the voyages of Columbus just before 1500. In a search for fortune, fame, adventure, and knowledge, Europeans began sailing the oceans. The American continents were the first and greatest discovery, but the New World was initially considered only an inconvenient obstacle in the way of the true goal—an easy sea route to the rich markets of the Orient.

The first Europeans since the Norsemen to enter arctic waters were English and Dutch adventurers looking for a shortcut to China. It was widely believed that a sea passage could be found either to the west above North America or to the east above Asia. For more than three hundred years explorers would search for the elusive Northwest and Northeast Passages.

Englishmen like Martin Frobisher and John Davis began the search by probing the complex maze of thousands of inlets, straits, and bays of the Canadian Arctic Islands in the late sixteenth century. During the arctic summers they sailed between the icebergs, but the onset of winter forced the explorers to leave or risk being trapped, their ships crushed by the grinding ice. In this way the mapping of the Arctic, piece by piece, was begun.

The expeditions of John Davis were particularly successful. He made three voyages in three years, from 1585 to 1587. In his small ships, *Sunneshine* and *Mooneshine,* Davis rediscovered Greenland and charted hundreds of miles of coastline. He made contact with native tribes, treating them with respect. He studied Inuit customs as well as arctic plants, animals, currents, and ice conditions before being forced home by the approach of winter each year.

Many expeditions followed those of the early pioneers. The search for a northern passage became a kind of quest. But the Arctic would not yield its secrets easily, and not all explorers enjoyed Davis's success.

In 1596 a Dutch expedition led by Willem Barents sailed above Europe in search of the Northeast Passage. Trapped in a jumble of ice floes, their ship was gradually crushed by the relentless pressure of the ice. The men escaped in small boats to a nearby island. There they built a shelter of driftwood where they lived in total isolation as winter closed in, bringing with it unending darkness and temperatures of fifty degrees below zero.

Without adequate clothing, and terrified by curious polar bears, the men survived for nine months by rationing their stores of salted meat. Barents's men developed scurvy, a disease brought on by the lack of vitamin C, which could cause bleeding gums, weakness, and eventually even death. They didn't know that the Inuit diet of raw meat and blubber would have prevented the disease.

When the ice finally began to break up in June, the company set out in two small boats across 1,600 miles of open ocean. During their ordeal, several men died of exposure, scurvy, and starvation, including Barents. The survivors were the first Europeans to live through an arctic winter. One of them wrote, "Men wondered to see us, having believed us long ago to have been dead and rotten."

In 1607 English explorer Henry Hudson tried a different route to the Pole. Instead of east or west, he sailed directly north. Hudson believed that he could push through the zone of ice and sail straight across the top of the world to the North Pole, a huge black stone emerging from a warm, calm sea. Of course, when Hudson encountered the ice pack east of Greenland, he was forced to retreat.

FOLLOWING PAGES: *Elizabethan ships sail among gigantic icebergs.*

Hudson made several more voyages, searching for both Passages. On a fateful expedition, this time to the northwest, Hudson's crew mutinied. The explorer, his young son, and five loyal crewmen were set adrift in a small boat without oars in the middle of a huge body of water that Hudson had discovered. They disappeared among the ice floes of Hudson Bay and were never seen again.

As the search for the mysterious Northwest and Northeast Passages continued throughout the seventeenth and eighteenth centuries, the map of the Arctic gradually began to fill in. Men like William Baffin, Robert Bylot, and Vitus Bering gave their names to the bays, islands, and straits that they discovered. But progress was very slow.

GEOGRAPHICAL EXPLORATION WAS not the only reason for voyages to the Arctic. Resources that supported the Inuit were also in high demand by Europeans, such as the luxurious fur of polar animals like sables and arctic foxes. By 1700 fur trading empires were growing in Russia and North America—by the mid–nineteenth century one-third of the Imperial Russian treasury came from the sale of Siberian furs.

The number of animals killed was staggering. Between 1770 and 1870 nearly eleven million skins were sold by the Hudson's Bay Company, one of the Canadian trading networks. As the remote trading posts and trapping territories were established, the unknown arctic interior was slowly exposed.

Meanwhile, whalers followed (and sometimes led) explorers into unknown seas, where they found vast herds of their prey. Whale blubber contains oil of the finest quality, used for lighting and heating in Europe and America in the time before petroleum was refined. Certain types of whales also provided *baleen,* fringed bony plates that some whales have for straining food from seawater. Baleen was used to make goods such as

Barents's men are terrified of curious polar bears.

umbrellas and corsets. For three centuries, year after year, scores of whaling ships entered the arctic seas. Using harpoons thrown from small boats, whalers slaughtered thousands of the great sea mammals, taking the parts they wanted and leaving the gigantic carcasses for the fish, sea birds, and polar bears. Many species of whales were hunted to the very edge of extinction.

Even the most famous explorers spent only a few summer seasons in the Arctic, but the anonymous fur trappers and whalers returned year after year, learning to live and work under extreme conditions.

As Europeans penetrated the far north, they came in contact more and more often with the Inuit. Diseases to which the native people had no resistance wiped out entire families and villages. In their attempt to conquer nature, Europeans brought their own ideas and technology to arctic survival; the Inuit, with their snow houses, fur clothing, dog sledges, kayaks, and diet of oily meat and raw blubber, were thought to have nothing to teach "civilized" men.

ON AUGUST 8, 1818, a British naval expedition led by John Ross encountered the Polar Inuit, a small group who lived in isolation in a game-rich region of northwest Greenland, farther north than any other people on earth. Terrified by the ships, which they took to be gigantic magic birds, the natives were astonished when the British officers appeared, shivering but impressive in their full-dress uniforms. "Do you come from the sun or from the moon?" wondered the Inuit, warm in their furs.

Ross's expedition was the first of many launched by the British navy after the Napoleonic wars in Europe. Large ships, idle in peacetime, were fully manned and provisioned for several years at sea. With more reliable ships and more accurate instruments,

Whaling was a dangerous business.

the nineteenth century marked a new, more scientific era of exploration.

In 1819 an expedition led by Sir William Parry was the first to intentionally spend the winter in the Arctic. Parry understood that the northern winter was not only physically dangerous, but that it was also hazardous to the spirit, with unending cold, darkness, boredom, and isolation. These conditions, combined with a poor diet of preserved food, could bring on a kind of madness called *arctic fever*. While they lived out the winter in relative safety in the shelter of the ice-bound ships, Parry made sure that his crew kept busy with scientific observations and repairs to the ships and equipment. He arranged theatrical evenings and musical performances—Parry himself played the violin. Even the local Inuit occasionally participated. The Northwest Passage remained undiscovered, but Parry went farther north and saw more of the Arctic than any explorer before him.

In 1845 Arctic veteran Sir John Franklin led a well-equipped expedition in two large ships with the ominous names *Terror* and *Erebus* (in Greek mythology, Erebus is the deepest, darkest part of the underworld). Charged with finding the Northwest Passage once and for all, Franklin and his crew of 129 men sailed into the icy labyrinth of islands and channels in northern Canada—and simply disappeared.

When the expedition did not return after two or three years as expected, the mystery of Franklin's fate captured the public imagination. During the 1850s more than forty separate expeditions entered the Arctic to find the answer. Several of these were organized by Franklin's wife, who refused to give up without knowing what had happened to her husband. Gradually the tragic story was pieced together.

In remote Victoria Strait, *Terror* and *Erebus* became hopelessly trapped in ice that did not break up when summer came. After two years Franklin died, the tinned food and salted meat began to run out, and arctic fever struck. The men abandoned ship and marched out over the ice dragging massive sledges and impossibly heavy boats loaded with useless things such as china place settings and fancy silverware. Exhausted, starving, weakened by scurvy, and poisoned by the lead in their improperly tinned food, the company struggled onward, leaving a grim trail of graves and, finally, individual corpses, frozen where they fell. There was even evidence of cannibalism. No one survived. It was the worst of all Arctic disasters.

Ironically, the scores of expeditions crisscrossing the region in search of Franklin opened up more of the Arctic than had been revealed in the previous three hundred years. Except for the remotest areas of northern Greenland and the Canadian Islands, the map of the arctic coastlines was almost completed. It was now understood that the ice-clogged Northwest Passage was simply too hazardous to be a practical shipping route.

The Siberian coastline is less rugged, however, and in the years 1878 and 1879 Swedish explorer N. A. E. Nordenskjöld succeeded in making the Northeast Passage in the *Vega,* a large sailing ship equipped with steam engines. Nordenskjöld was made a baron by the Swedish government for his accomplishment, one of the great voyages in arctic history. In the twentieth century, with the development of powerful ice-breaking ships, Nordenskjöld's route became a major shipping lane.

The Northwest Passage was not completed until after the turn of the century, when Norwegian explorer Roald Amundsen spent the years 1903 to 1906 inching a small sailing vessel, the *Gjøa,* through the entire length of the torturous route. After three centuries of exploration, the great puzzle of the northern passages was finally solved.

AT ITS VERY center, the Arctic held an even greater enigma. The polar sea covers

FOLLOWING PAGES: *Franklin's men abandon their ships, dragging heavy sledges and boats over the ice.*

nearly five million square miles. Except for its southernmost fringes, this vast area was totally unknown. At the end of the nineteenth century the focus of exploration shifted to the Arctic Ocean and its farthest point—the North Pole.

The great pioneer in this endeavor was a brilliant young Norwegian scientist named Fridtjof Nansen. Also an athlete, outdoorsman, artist, and poet, Nansen wrote of the strange atmospheric effect called the *northern lights,* "The aurora borealis shakes over the vault of heaven its veil of glittering silver—changing now to yellow, now to green, now to red. . . . It shimmers in tongues of flame . . . until the whole melts away in the moonlight . . . like the sigh of a departing spirit."

In 1888, at the age of twenty-six, Nansen organized his first expedition—a trek across Greenland on skis, a feat never before accomplished. Dropped off by ship on the uninhabited east coast, Nansen and five companions had no choice but to ski westward to civilization, carrying only the provisions required for the one-way journey.

This kind of bold yet calculated risk-taking was typical of Nansen. He carefully planned every detail, even designing his own equipment. He also knew how to improvise off the land, adopting Inuit methods such as the use of dog sledges, kayaks, and snow houses.

After the Greenland trek, Nansen became interested in the idea of *polar drift.* In 1884, in the ice near Greenland, some debris was found from the *Jeannette,* a ship crushed in the ice off Siberia in 1881. There was only one possible explanation: the ice and debris had drifted around the entire Arctic Ocean. Nansen had a breathtaking proposal: he would sail a ship directly into the ice pack off Siberia, deliberately let it be frozen in, and drift with the ice across the top of the world, penetrating the heart of the Arctic.

Fridtjof Nansen and the Fram

Nansen's small ship, the *Fram* (*Onward* in Norwegian), was specially designed with a hull that would ride up over the crushing ice and living spaces insulated with cork and felt. Fully provisioned with scientific equipment and supplies for five years, the *Fram* had workshops, a smithy, and even a windmill for electricity. On June 24, 1893, the *Fram* sailed from Norway. By September 25, Nansen and his crew of twelve were frozen fast in the polar ice pack off Siberia.

As they drifted slowly northward, the expedition settled into a routine of scientific observation. The ship was so comfortable that by the end of the second winter Nansen was restless and bored. Now only 360 miles from the North Pole, Nansen decided to strike out over the ice.

In the arctic dawn of mid-March 1895 Nansen set out with one companion, Hjalmar Johansen, three sledges of provisions, twenty-eight dogs, and two kayaks. As in Greenland, there could be no turning back—this time their home base was drifting. For three weeks they struggled northward, maneuvering the sledges over jumbled fields and immense ridges of broken ice. By early April they were still 225 miles from the Pole, and the drifting ice was carrying them south almost as quickly as they could push north. Provisions were also running low, so they reluctantly headed for the nearest land, three hundred miles to the south. As the weeks passed and the sun rose higher, the broken surface of the ice pack became slushy, then treacherous as lanes of water called *leads* opened and closed between the ice floes. It took four months to reach land. After provisions ran out, the men survived by hunting seals in the open leads and by feeding the weak dogs to the stronger ones.

Nansen and Johansen finally found a remote island. With no hope of rescue, the two men prepared for the winter, building a tiny hut and butchering walrus and bears for a supply of meat and warm furs. They survived the winter in isolation, burning greasy blubber for heat and light and growing fat on the diet of oily meat. When the ice broke up in the spring, Nansen and Johansen set out in their kayaks. On June 13, 1896—one year and four months after leaving the *Fram*—they were picked up by an English expedition. Two months later the *Fram* and its crew broke free of the ice in the ocean east of Greenland, more than a thousand miles from their starting point. The scientific expedition was a triumphant success, and Nansen and Johansen had gone farther north than anyone had before.

Now the race to the North Pole was on. Another daring attempt was made the very next year—a flight to the Pole in a balloon. Salomon Andrée was a Swedish engineer with experience in aeronautics and an interest in the Arctic. He had built a large hydrogen-filled balloon with a passenger gondola designed to hold three men, four months of supplies, sledges, and a small boat.

Developed more than one hundred years earlier, balloons were still the only means of flight in the 1890s. As transportation they have serious limitations: first, they cannot be steered; and second, they are sensitive to temperature changes. Andrée tried to solve the first problem with a complicated system of sails and drag lines. He completely ignored the second problem, and the result was disastrous.

In midsummer 1897 the *Ornen* (*Eagle* in Swedish) lifted off from Spitsbergen, an island north of Norway. As they sailed northward Andrée wrote in his journal, "The rattling of the drag lines in the snow and the flapping of the sails are the only sound, except for the whining of the wind." As the balloon was alternately heated by the sun and cooled by freezing fog, the precious gas that kept them aloft leaked away. By the third day the *Ornen* was down on the ice, two hundred miles from land. In the arctic summer

FOLLOWING PAGES: *The* Fram *drifts in the Arctic night. Ice crystals in the air cause lunar halos, and the aurora borealis flickers overhead.*

at the edge of the ice pack, Andrée and his two companions faced a terrifying world of slushy, grinding floes and open leads; it took them three months to struggle to the nearest island. But inexperienced and unprepared, they were unable to survive the winter. We know what happened only because thirty-three years later their frozen remains were found, along with Andrée's journal and another eerie relic—undeveloped images of the doomed expedition that were still in their camera.

PHYSICALLY THE NORTH Pole is nothing more than a theoretical point on the earth's surface—but reaching it came to symbolize mankind's mastery of the entire planet—and a landmark human achievement. An American naval engineer desperately wanted to be the first explorer to stand on the North Pole. Robert E. Peary first entered the Arctic in 1886. For twenty years he mounted expeditions to northwest Greenland, looking for the best route north. Peary was not particularly interested in scientific discovery or mapping. He had one goal: the glory of being first. Over the years, Peary came to believe that it was his destiny to conquer the North Pole.

Vain and arrogant, Robert Peary ran his expeditions like a military campaign. His chief lieutenant was his personal assistant, Matthew Henson, a man of African descent. This was unusual at the turn of the century, but then, Peary was unconventional in many ways. He also took his wife on some of his early expeditions. Josephine Peary was the first white woman in the High Arctic, and she gave birth to their daughter while on expedition. Inuit came from miles around to see the newborn blond "snowbaby."

As an explorer, Peary was innovative, taking ideas from everyone and improving on them. But the Polar Inuit were the key to his success. Inuit women made his furs and Inuit men used their own dogs to pull his sledges. They built his snowhouses on the trail

The Ornen *comes down on the ice.*

and hunted for his meat in exchange for metal tools and other material goods. On one occasion Peary pushed himself so relentlessly that his feet froze. When his fur boots were removed, several of his toes snapped off. As soon as the stumps healed, he was back on the trail.

In 1906 Peary made a full-scale assault upon the North Pole. His plan was to take a ship as far north as possible, winter over in Greenland or the Canadian Islands, then strike out for the Pole in late February, before the ice pack started breaking up. The Arctic did not cooperate, however. When only a hundred miles out on the ice pack, the expedition was delayed several days by a broad lead, then a blizzard kept them camp-bound for another week. Supplies dwindled, and the disappointed Peary had to settle for a new farthest north record, 175 miles from the Pole.

After another appeal to the men who financed his expeditions, Peary sailed from New York in July 1908 in the *Roosevelt,* named for Theodore Roosevelt, then president of the United States and the explorer's most enthusiastic supporter. Peary was fifty-two years old, and he knew that this was his last expedition.

But Peary was not the only explorer in the Arctic in 1908. There was also Dr. Frederick A. Cook, a veteran of both the Arctic and the Antarctic, which was just then being explored. Cook had been the physician on one of Peary's earlier expeditions. Always jealous and overbearing, Peary had refused to allow Cook to publish an article about his experiences and they had quarreled. Now the doctor was rumored to be thinking about his own attempt on the North Pole. Peary dismissed the rumors; he considered Cook an amateur, not in the same league as himself.

On March 1, 1909, Peary stood on the frozen shore of the Arctic Ocean and faced north. With him were 23 men, 19 sledges, and 133 dogs. For the next month Matt

Henson led out in front, breaking trail, while Peary rode a sledge in the rear, supervising the troops. Other sledges traveled back and forth relaying tons of supplies northward, provisions for the return trip that were stored in snowhouses strung out over almost five hundred miles of floating, shifting ice. Everything had been carefully calculated, down to the sacrificing of weak dogs to feed the strong.

For the final dash to the Pole, Peary took only Henson and three Inuit; he was reluctant to share the glory with another white man. The entry in his diary for April 6, 1909, reads, "The Pole at last!!! The prize of 3 centuries, my dream & ambition for 23 years. MINE at last."

Or was it?

PEARY CAME HOME to the stunning news that Dr. Cook had already returned, claiming to have reached the North Pole on April 21, 1908, a year before Peary. In the investigations that followed, Peary accused Cook of lying, and it was demonstrated that Cook had lied once before when he claimed to have climbed Mt. McKinley in Alaska, North America's highest peak. Lacking documentation or witnesses, except for two Inuit companions who said they were never out of sight of land, Cook's claim to have reached the Pole was officially rejected.

Then, incredibly, Peary was also unable to completely verify his own claim. The careful explorer was a sloppy navigator, and from his solar observations and daily journal it was impossible to say that he had stood at the Pole. Henson and the Inuit were unable to take solar readings, so it was Peary's word against Cook's. Commander Robert E. Peary was finally given the credit and made a rear-admiral, but his great prize was tar-

FOLLOWING PAGES: *Dog sledging on the ice pack*

nished and he died an embittered man. As for Cook, he vowed until his dying day that he had reached the North Pole. In recent years, historical researchers have determined that neither man actually stepped foot on the northernmost point of the globe.

THE CLASSIC ERA of Arctic exploration ended with Peary. Attention then shifted to the Antarctic and to the South Pole, which Roald Amundsen reached in 1911. Three years later the world was at war and most exploration was postponed. When it resumed in the 1920s the world was a different place. Balloons were no longer the only means of flight, and several attempts were made to fly to the North Pole in small airplanes.

For many years Richard E. Byrd was given credit for the first successful flight, but his claim is now disputed. In 1926 Roald Amundsen flew across the entire Arctic Ocean in an Italian dirigible piloted by its designer, Umberto Nobile. The first person to stand at the North Pole, whose claim is undisputed, is Joseph Fletcher, a United States Air Force pilot who landed there in 1952. Arctic flights are great achievements, but they are achievements of technology, somehow different from crossing nearly five hundred miles of shifting ice by dog sledge and then returning. Although many people have now stood at the North Pole, no one has ever completed Peary's journey without being resupplied by plane or airlifted out.

During the last half of the twentieth century, the modern world has entered the Arctic. Powerful icebreakers keep shipping lanes open, airliners fly over the Arctic Ocean, and nuclear submarines cruise under the ice pack. Nations search for valuable mineral resources, and scientific research stations and military installations have been permanently established. The American base in remote northern Greenland was even given Pytheas's poetic name *Thule.*

Peary claims the North Pole.

Our presence in the Arctic has changed the lives of the Inuit as well. Most now live in prefabricated houses, watch television, and drive snowmobiles. Like people else-where, they have become dependent on modern technology, and for better or worse, the old ways are kept alive only by individual Inuit with an interest in their rich ancient heritage.

Mysterious and forbidding, the Arctic remains one of the last great wildernesses, still hiding secrets waiting to be discovered. As recently as 1978, a small rocky speck of land was detected under the ice off the northern coast of Greenland. Named in honor of one of the Inuit who accompanied Peary on his final expedition, the tiny island of *Oodaaq* is the northernmost land on earth—until our next journey into the ice.

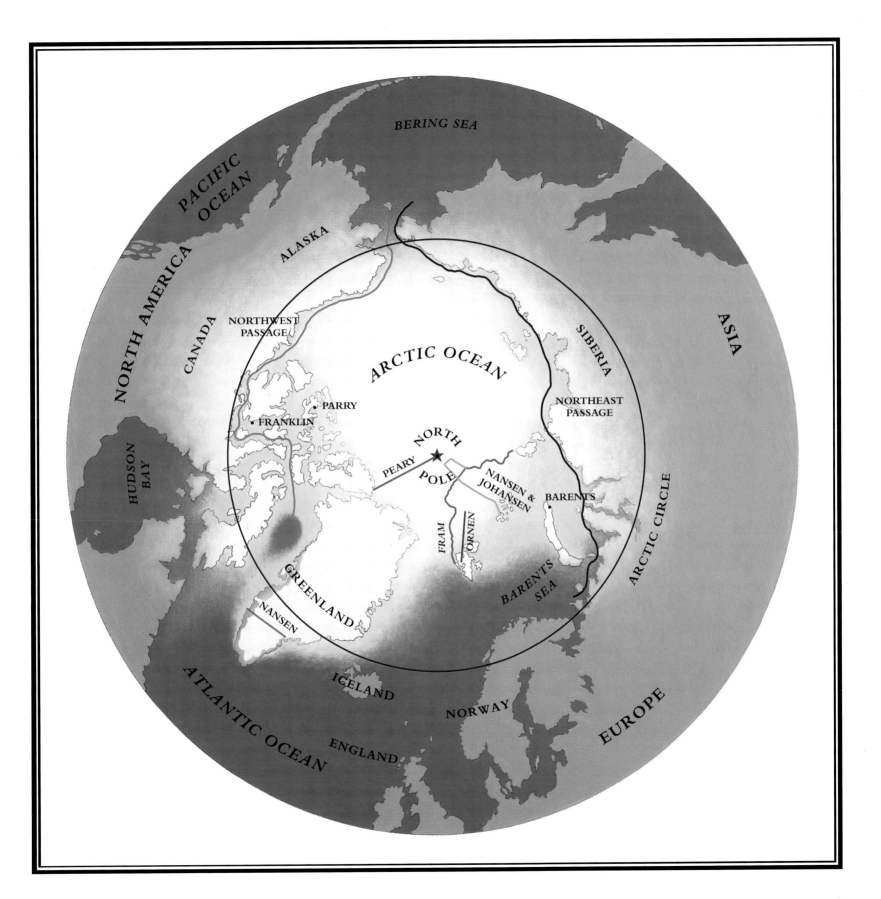

TIME LINE

10,000–5,000 B.C. The last Ice Age ends and people gradually enter the Arctic. Their descendants become the Inuit.

EARLY VOYAGES

330 B.C. Pytheas sails to Thule

A.D. 550 Saint Brendan's voyage

950–1150 Norsemen sail west

THE AGE OF DISCOVERY

1492 Columbus's first voyage

1576 Frobisher first enters the Arctic

1585–87 Davis's Expeditions

1595–96 Barents's ordeal

1607–11 Hudson searches for a passage

1600–1900 The great era of whaling and fur trading

THE CLASSIC ERA OF POLAR EXPLORATION

1818 Ross commands the first British naval expedition

1819–20 Parry winters over

1845–47 The doomed Franklin expedition

1850s Many expeditions search for Franklin

1878–79   Nordenskjöld makes the Northeast Passage

1888   Nansen crosses Greenland

1893–96   The drift of the *Fram*

1897   The flight of the *Ornen*

1903–1906   Amundsen sails the Northwest Passage

1906   Peary's first assault on the Pole

1908   Cook claims the Pole

1909   Peary claims the Pole

1920s   First flights in the Arctic

BIBLIOGRAPHY

Berton, Pierre. *The Arctic Grail.* New York: Viking, 1988.

Bruemmer, Fred. *The Arctic World.* San Francisco: Sierra Club, 1985.

Bryce, Robert M. *Cook & Peary: The Polar Controversy, Resolved.* Mechanicsburg, Penn.: Stackpole Books, 1997.

Herbert, Wally. *The Noose of Laurels: Robert E. Peary and the Race for the North Pole.* New York: Doubleday, 1989.

Lopez, Barry. *Arctic Dreams.* New York: Charles Scribner's Sons, 1986.

Mountfield, David. *A History of Polar Exploration.* New York: Dial, 1974.

Nansen, Fridtjof. *Farthest North.* New York: Harper & Brothers, 1897.

Payne, Lee. *Lighter Than Air: An Illustrated History of the Airship.* New York: Orion Books, 1977.

Shackleton, Edward. *Nansen the Explorer.* London: H. F. & G. Witherby, 1959.

Weems, J. E. *Peary: The Explorer and the Man.* Boston: Houghton Mifflin, 1967.

QUOTATION SOURCES

Barents quotation: Mountfield, p. 39

Nansen quotation: Nansen, v.I, p. 253

Andrée quotation: Payne, p. 23

Peary quotation: Herbert, p. 18

FURTHER READING

Anderson, Madelyn Klein. *Robert E. Peary and the Fight for the North Pole.* New York: Franklin Watts, 1992.

Beattie, Owen, and John Geiger. *Buried in Ice: The Mystery of a Lost Arctic Expedition.* New York: Scholastic Inc., 1992.

Ferris, Jeri. *Arctic Explorer: The Story of Matthew Henson.* Minneapolis: Carolrhoda Books, 1989.

George, Jean Craighead. *Julie of the Wolves.* New York: Harper & Row, 1972.

Jacobs, Francine. *A Passion for Danger: Nansen's Arctic Adventures.* New York: Putnam Publishing Group, 1994.

Kalman, Bobbie. *The Arctic Land.* New York: Crabtree Publishing Company, 1988.

MacInnis, Jeff, and Wade Rowland. *Polar Passage.* New York: Ballantine Books, 1989.

INDEX